# The Reach of Song

# 2021

*Steven Owen Shields*, Editor

*From chips and shards in idle times*

*I made these stories, shaped these rhymes;*

*May they engage some friendly tongue*

*When I am past the reach of song.*

Byron Herbert Reece

# Contents

*Prize Poems*

*In memoriam*

Dr. Robert L. Lynn

And

Ron W. Self

# The Byron Herbert Reece International Poetry Award

**Sponsor:**      The Georgia Poetry Society, in honor of Byron Herbert Reece, whose north Georgia upbringing informed five volumes of poetry on themes of nature and the Bible.  The competition was open to GPS members and non-members.

**Judge:**      Julie E. Bloemeke, Atlanta, GA

**1st Place:**      **The Ocean of That Night**
*David Hutto*

**2nd Place:**      **Surely I Heard It**
*Lynn Farmer*

**3rd Place:**      **Route One Memories**
*Kimberly J. Simms*

**HM:**      **White Cotillion**
*Clela Reed*

**HM:**      **Shoot Me Early On**
*Jill Jennings*

*David Hutto*

## The Ocean of That Night

In the yellow heat of summer days
when watermelon bacchanals
burst forth beneath the pecan trees,
I saw her late one summer afternoon.
She wore a dress of faded lace
and distant wild-night memories,
with earrings made of starlight
that fell on ripened corn.
She was drinking dreams from Mason jars,
whiskey smooth as true desire
and dark as ten-year wisdom.

As grasshoppers hummed the hymns
of Jesus in the field,
I asked if I could sit there on the porch.
I knew that most of life is made
of lies as big as planets,
but planets that can be worth living on.
And the lie I loved most dearly,
like vanilla on my lips,
was that I'd found a place to stay awhile.

We lazed along that afternoon,
where the quiet hounds of history
lounged cool beneath the endless shady porch,
and a mockingbird sang all the songs
of an entire music school.
She talked of southern gardens,

about quail and muscadines,
and how to make the moonlight change its shape.
Twisting Celtic patterns
seemed to wrap her DNA
with every song the green isle ever knew.

When twilight came she led me back
through rooms of restless spirits
of people who had dreamed across that land.
She took out another bottle
from Kentucky full of sin
as sweet as honeysuckle on God's throne.
There were fireflies out the window
like an ocean of desire,
and all night long we sounded Heaven's thunder.

When the sunlight came with biscuits,
fig preserves, and salted ham,
she asked me if I like how fiddles sound.
She put on an old scratched record,
and musicians from the twenties
walked through that room with tunes of love gone wrong.
I wish I lived again back then,
back in that sapphire morning,
and when I hear a fiddle
crying notes and moaning fire,
I ache like lonely water
for the ocean of that night.

*Lynn Farmer*

---

## Surely I Heard It

The silence thunders around me
in its miracle cadence
with an easily hidden music,
as I am beckoned to slow and listen
for what I often miss in the noise
of day to day:

the slight rustle of leaves,
as a certain breeze passes through
their yellow fingers;

a single branch falling
beyond the path into its own
emptiness;

the crunch and crackle of other
dried and cast off sticks
and acorns at my feet;

the stones of the path beneath,
no easier to walk this day than ever.

And suddenly, I'm shaken back
from nature to the world
of our creation
by the consistent hum of the air
at the back of the building;
the whine of an engine
beyond the first colored hill;

and the cool roar of the silver plane
above, taking someone where
she thought she wanted
to go to get away.

But then, I rest in the assurance
that all is well and will be.
I turn at the slightest sound—
the soft patter of the little red dog
and a lone bird's singing—
surely I heard it, somewhere,
maybe there, off in the forest
and beckoning me to listen still.

*Kimberly J. Simms*

## Route One Memories

We are falling up, riding altocumuli
driving Route One in a 280Z,
curving. Car same blue-green as the sea.
We hush onto the road shoulder, a payphone,
you call home the Pacific conducting
its spray symphony before you, Redwood

trees at your back. Port town we eat Dungeness
crabs, wind driving our cheeks red, as we spoon
chowder into mouths singing of the sea.
In our turreted Victorian B&B
we are greedy for the sunset waves
thrashing the mica-flecked pebbles. We drive

on up Shasta mountains, churn over ridges
lined with fire-black carcasses of trees.
We turn the curve, a forest of windmills

on the step, thousands of turning blades sing.
Singing clear-skyed future on pearlescent wings.

*Clela Reed*

## White Cotillion

Just as the green of tree and hedge
loses its pale-gold shimmer,
deepens into lush backdrop,
the maidens of spring
burst forth in white dresses,
at once both cool and hot,
shy and brazen.

Daisies spark the hills and fields,
       ready for chains
       and children's bouquets,
playing their peasant abundance to cheery effect,
and Queen Anne's Lace nod their galaxy heads
beside the busy road,
pretending to be more than
       wild carrots,
offering their multitudinous stars
in Chantilly patterns as pedigree proof.

Gardenias and Magnolias, the debutantes
in satin dresses, compete in fragrance
       after opening slowly,
       teasing attention,
       flouncing their *peau de soie* petals
       against polished leaves,
as they perfume the air for their suitors.

But the Oak Leaf Hydrangea has no such airs,
sending her musty smell into the woods,
crocheting four-petaled clusters
          into big granny gowns and shifts,
lifting her green-tinged whiteness
          away from hungry deer.
Honest and open, the lassie next door,
she feeds the bees and insects.
She knows her place in the world.

*Jill Jennings*

## Shoot Me Early On

Somebody out there, please tell me
before I make a fool of myself
the way our former governor did
when a reporter asked him a reasonable
question in a TV interview.
He'd been such a good public servant, reduced now
to this wild-eyed *has-been* spewing AM radio
soundbites in an argument no one could even follow.
I was so embarrassed for him.

Somebody push me off the stage,
knock me down if need be,
tell the audience there's a security
threat, do whatever you have to
to keep me from standing at some
podium saying ah ah ah,
my eyes closed as I try to remember
the title of my first book,
scratching my white haired
head with a knobby arthritic

finger as I waste time stalling,
then ranting on and on
like Clint Eastwood at the
2012 Republican National
Convention, when everyone
laughed but no one really got it.

Shoot me with a dart gun
if you have to, but keep
me out of the public eye
when I get so old I can't read
from one of my own books
except *sotto voce,*
with a trembling hand, eventually
dropping the volume facedown
on the floor.

Get to me before I reach down
to pick it up and fall head-first
into the orchestra pit.
Tell me when my arms are too flabby
to wear a sleeveless dress on camera,
and for God's sake make
the time out T sign if I ever
start rambling on about my ailments!

I don't want to turn into
one of those precious dears
with the shuffling gait
of Tim Conway and the fervid
eyes of a skinhead anarchist
trying to perform my poems
while the folks sitting
in the front row look at each other
and say:
*She used to be quite a speaker,
a good poet in her day,* and then pronounce
the fatal words: *bless her heart!*

# The Ira E. Harrison Social Issues Poetry Award

**Sponsor:** The Georgia Poetry Society, in honor of past GPS President Ira E. Harrison, author of *Poetry and Prevention; B.A.A.D. Beautiful African-American Daughters: Poems of Tribute.* This competition was open to GPS members and non-members.

**Judge:** Barry Marks, Birmingham, AL

**1st Place:** **To Open: A User's Manual**
*Clela Reed*

**2nd Place:** **#metoo**
*Donna Rose Mulcahy*

**3rd Place:** **Season of the Moon**
*Nancy Cook*

**HM:** **Movin' Toward Tomorrow**
*Lou Jones*

**HM:** **trigger: early notification of auto insurance payment due**
*doris davenport*

*Clela Reed*

## To Open:  A User's Manual

~1~
Hands

First, unfurl the fists.
Free each finger, starting
with the index (much better
at pointing to a sunset,
pressing a doorbell)
and ending with the pinkie,
which always hid, anyway.
Now use them
to pet, to clap,
to knead the dough.
Give something away.
Feed the birds. Wave.
Now receive the apple,
the present, the rose.
Watch them carry. Watch them lift.
Behold the world they can hold.

~2~
Mind

Start with light.
Let it reach into the depths
where bias squats and frets.
Read a book. Write a poem.
Listen to the homeless woman
who greets you each day at the corner.
Honor science as you would a parent.
Crack the rusty notions that bind your gears.
Banish those nibbling vermin, your fears.

Travel. Sing a song from another land.
Now look at those you thought were odd
and find instead iterations of God.

~3~
Heart

Begin with breath.
Breathe in peace; breathe out love.
Repeat until you've filled the room,
the city, the cosmos.
Keep breathing.
Mind the muscular beat.
Drum empathy until the chambers,
the very vaults expand wide,
welcoming into the halls of atria
both the suffering and the celebrants.


Remain open. Wait to be filled.

## Donna Rose Mulcahy

**#metoo**

1 boy, 2 girls

College interns on the Hill, Carlo Rossi Chablis
Let's play naked cards, says she.
We agree amidst the charged laughter
of the barely-out-of-their-teens.
Soon she will go to bed carelessly,
leaving me alone,
pinned underneath.

You walk around with those things,
looking for a warm place.
Believe you come in peace,
leave hollows in your wake.

1 girl is no match

He enters without knocking,
without warning.
The shock clamps the air
around me. I am still.

At your disposal, an arsenal of fists
for words and dick,
the weapon of choice irrelevant

Corpulent jock always plays for the winning team

      The assembly of unanswered no's
      amplify, threaten to shatter me.
      They gain strength,
      take hold.
      Breathe on their own.

            Who am I but someone for you to
            plow through?
            What is left when you claim victory,
            take all the pieces and go home?

What did I expect?

      He stands down, removes his weapon.
      Re-affixes his mask.
      Joins the ranks
      of upstanding citizen rapists in the neighborhood.

            Years later, searching still
            for some small retreat,
            we grow louder.
            Does it matter?

*Nancy Cook*

## Season of the Moon

Night dresses in Dawn's colors.
This heat is orange. Inescapable.
Aspens don't move a muscle.
Mountain laurels hold their breath.
In the meadow, turkeys raise
a clatter but make no sound,
muffled by the fire's drumbeat.

Shadows of light-hoofed deer
clear the boundary fence.
In the face of angry winds,
eight hundred villagers flee.
There is but one road out. Only
Hermit Jack stands his ground.
Pistol in hand. He'll die here.

If the end ever comes, cold light
will follow rain. The long nights
of flame and fear will leave behind
on car and truck carcasses, on
scattered stone and remnant
steel, deep drifts of fallen ash.
It will be as snow on the moon.

# Lou Jones

## Movin' Toward Tomorrow

*We did not see him again. Perhaps the desire to go home had been greater than the wish to go North to freedom. Or perhaps he had been afraid to travel with us by daylight. Or suspicious of our offer. Or maybe [...]*
*~Langston Hughes, Forward From Life (The Lost Essay)*

Ed Pinkney hands the rooming housekeeper a note and a dollar
  bill:
*Please see that Mr. Pinkney is up and ready to leave at 6:00 AM,*
*when Miss Hurston and I come for him. The dollar is for a bath and*
*boiling his clothing. Thank you.*
*Langston Hughes.*

The chain gang runaway sits naked on a canvas cot, eating a piece of
pone cake, rested, precious hours of sleep after two days on the run.
No more sleepin' in a cage, captured by shackles, no night chorus of
clanging chains, convicts shifting on straw mattresses, cursing,
sobbing and incanting prayers, swatting flies and mosquitoes —no
stench rising from the steaming bodies of unwashed men.

Ed regrets lyin' to those fine New York people. His guilt places the lie
on a scale with stealin' and cheatin', a stain on his record, for sure.
Many black brothers and sisters are fleein' the Jim Crow South,
goin' North, wantin' a better life. Now is not his time, not goin'
without his new wife, not makin' the trip with those Harlem folks,
jammed in with baggage in their little car, no sir, not riskin' bein'
spotted by some keen-eyed deputy on the lookout for footloose
  Negroes.

The lad stares out the window into the Low Country darkness, sky alive
with stars, his mind caught up in the challenge of the journey ahead.
Atlanta, hoofin' it all the way, not hidin' roadside lookin' for rides,
puttin' himself in plain view sittin' next to a black sharecropper in his
mule wagon, no sir, too risky. He'll be hikin' the back road darkness,
makin' it through the pines and hardwoods in the light of day, goin' for
his bride — she not knowing where he is, if she'll ever see him again.

Pinkney finishes the cake, slips into his damp trousers, picks up his
shirt and laceless brogans, walks softly up the hallway, quietly
opens the door and steps outside. The grass is heavy with dew, his
   torso is
swabbed by the thick night air, mind workin' hard as he slides along
the shadows of the two-story clapboard house. He steps into his boots,
walks briskly, charged with purpose, a lone figure on Savannah
side streets and alleys, advancing against sunrise, movin', headin' to
the outskirts before dawn breathes life into the city.

Ed is deep in the pines by sunup, before cars, trucks, and wagons are
ownin' the roads, before chain gangs are scoopin' out roadside ditches,
guards on watch, rifles cradled in their arms. He's on the move, workin'
his plan, he'll be takin' back roads at night, movin' through forests and
clean-picked cotton fields in daylight, followin' the sun. Livin' on
wild berries and pecans, vegetable gardens, drinkin' from
fresh streams and mule troughs, gettin' by with little rest.

Not goin' back to no chain gang, whipped with a knotted strap,
trussed around a post, head to knees, faintin' face down in the
red Georgia dust, no sir. No more chains and shackles, caged like
an animal. Stakin' his fate on movin', runnin' til he can't run no more,
felled by effort, on his knees begging favor, believing he matters,
that God cares.

The young fugitive continues through the woods, breathing freedom, his heart tied to the spirit-weary black brothers he left behind, toiling sunrise to sunset, under the whip, broken on the rack — proud men stripped of dignity, purgatoried in a world of lost selves, where time moves no faster than the moment. He's movin', movin', fueled by resolve, certain the day is coming when the black man will no longer abide such treatment.

*doris davenport*

---

## trigger: early notification of auto insurance payment due
*(A Meditation on Driving-While-Black, deemed a crime by Systemic-Whyte-Supremacy)*

if i could, i would just
park it. Park it and leave it
my beloved vintage 2004 Toyota, Zora,
parked. no more insurance no more changes no

driving-while-black ("dwb") probable or possible death
by whytemale sadists no need to neck swivel left, right,
as, paranoid, drive below speed limits park and walk
park and read, nap park and sit in my car like it is my

living room like we did in Granddaddy John's
old Chevy for privacy for fun maybe practice
my dulcimer can't get fined yet for that (*ikr?* "I know, right")
sing a rhythm of no rules no traffic no fees no

punishment, no insurance just me and
my Zora out here under
the trees crooning (DAD dulcimer tabs)
park it. park it. Oh, park it.

# The Nonce-Sense Poetry Award

**Sponsor:** The Georgia Poetry Society. This competition challenged entrants to submit a poem in an invented, or "nonce," form.

**Judge:** Jeff Hardin, Columbia, TN

**1ˢᵗ Place:** **The Elderly Monk Explains to His Pupil Five Paths to Enlightenment**
*David Hutto*

**2ⁿᵈ Place:** **Last Lay for Sylvia and Ted**
*Robert Wyatt*

**3ʳᵈ Place:** **Parallel Lines**
*Jill Jennings*

**HM:** **The Discussion of Nonce at the Poetry Roundtable—A Calzone**
*Randy Mazie*

*David Hutto*

## The Elderly Monk Explains to His Pupil Five Paths to Enlightenment

The Master said:
One time I walked on the sun.
An ocean of crimson and purple fire
swirled around my feet.
Flaming mountains rose and fell,
rose up, and fell again,
as vast as the Himalayas.
I heard a rumble
like the coughing of God,
and jets of fire shot into space.
From those furnace towers a thousand miles high,
radio waves carried the sound of light into the darkness.

The pupil glanced up at the bright sun, then looked down.

The Master said:
One time I walked at the bottom of the sea.
I went to observe life where life began,
deep in the great vast mother of all blue colors.
A cloud of tiny fish,
in green and gold,
flowed in dim sunlight all around me.
I walked through a forest of tall seaweed,
while up above, white octopi,
like undulating stars,
swam off.

The warm water grew colder the farther I walked,
and pious whales sang songs to celebrate their gods.

The pupil remembered walking along a beach and picking up a shell.

The Master said:
One time I walked along a strand of DNA.
Occasional photons of light
flashing through cell walls
lit the way ahead of me.
Atoms were like vibrating jewels
covered with sparks,
while electrons swarmed around me,
the flying stars of that cellular universe.
As I walked along, the DNA twisted and coiled like living ropes,
opening up just as waves on the ocean will separate
and come together again.
I had to watch my step
to keep from falling into the void.

The pupil heard the distant sound of monkeys in the forest.

The Master said:
One time I walked across a black hole far off in space.
Light was pouring in from all directions,
turning into vast streams of rainbows
that collapsed into a swirling ocean of light only one centimeter
    deep
I waded through the light,
surprised how weightless I felt.
Visions of the past moved in that shallow ocean
and I watched the universe begin,
over and over, like a movie.

Sounds from the universe
also fell into the black hole,
where they came together as one sound,
like slow, deep chanting.

The pupil felt a longing to be looking up at the night sky.

The Master said:
One time I walked through a door in time.
Standing at the door were ghosts,
who turned into people speaking,
surrounded by thousands of others.
There was a multitude of faces quickly changing as I moved into
    the past.
Lost possibilities flashed around me,
shimmering like layers of reality
that almost became real,
then faded.
And the souls of the dead continued to approach me with prayers
    in their mouths.

The pupil blinked and lowered his head.
"Master," he said, "this all sounds very difficult."

A slight smile appeared on the Master's face.
"I did not mean these are the only paths," he said.
"There are many others.
When you are ready,
you will begin to walk."

# Robert Wyatt

## Last Lay for Sylvia and Ted

*(n.b.: This is a "gender mirror" poem. Read middle and left columns for her perspective; the middle and right columns, for his.)*

*Making love with you*

| | |
|---|---|
| for the first time | still moves me physically. |
| after many months apart, | But seeing you again |

*evokes so many memories*

| | |
|---|---|
| and reassures me that | of torment and heartache |
| what we have is special. | that quenched my love for you. |

*Now I know for sure*

| | |
|---|---|
| that we will be together, | that I have made |
| despite all our problems, | an unalterable choice |

*for the intangible future.*

| | |
|---|---|
| Everything will be | I will return to her |
| as it was before. | and the child we have made. |

*We two fit together*

| | |
|---|---|
| like stanzas of a sonnet | well carnally and poetically, |
| we have written jointly. | but not as constant lovers. |

*I am no longer whole*

| | |
|---|---|
| without you and can't go on | without her, and so |
| bereft of your love. | *our* story has ended. |

*Jill Jennings*

## Parallel Lines

*Good neighbors good fences make. I take my stolen goods there for secret's sake.*

O, that this too, too solid ice might melt, that I may scuffle
    off to daily toil,
having loosed the tire chains that clang and bind.

Love is not lust from which true hormone wavers.

My lover's lips are nothing like the sun; her eyes when
    overdrunk are two fried eggs
about to run.

My Homey, O Homey, o, where are you roaming? Wait! I see
    your eyes are in the cut-up
sky.

Do not forsake me, o my fickle one.  I think you're mad from
    taking overmuch of sun.

What's in a rose? Does any other name, once proffered, smell
    as sweet?
Or will it sound like sirens singing through their nose?

The first time today the sun rose on you, love, I looked
    skyward to the moon
to slack your sleep

which was, alas, too bright for love to keep.  In short, I woke
you up.

When you to the summons of sweet talk, I gather up my
    courage to reply, I find
you are not listening. Goodbye.

*Randy Mazie*

## The Discussion of Nonce at the Poetry Roundtable—A Calzone*

*So what makes a poem nonce?*
        A student of Ogden Nash asked once.

*That's exactly it,* Nash said.
        The student stared and scratched his head.

Shel Silverstein rose up from his chair,
        adding, *I see nonce everywhere,*

to Nash's, *That's exactly it.*
        Dorothy Parker chimed in, *Kismet.*

*Truly,* Nash lovingly responded to her wit
        and once again exclaimed, *That's exactly it!*

Eve Merriam bellowed,  *How insightful,*
        *but I believe all your explanations are frightful.*

*What makes a poem nonce,*
        *none of you have answered once.*

*That's exactly it!* Nash said.
        Eve replied, *Nash, You're quite the knucklehead!*

*The answer to: What is nonce?*
        She shrugged, and said, *Not once.*

*Then it's twice,* Nash replied. *That's exactly it!*
        And that was all the discussion that he would permit.

* A *calzone* is a common, but complex, centuries-old Italian verse form which may have any number of lines, rhymed or not, and any meter, regular or irregular, but must include references to at least three or more well-known poets, and must have a phrase beginning in the third line of the poem that is irregularly repeated throughout the poem, whether at the beginning, middle or the end of the line. A calzone typically poses a question that demands an answer, but may not be ultimately apparent to anyone even at the end of the poem—which is why the style has continued on as long as it has.

# The Reigning Cats and Dogs Poetry Award

**Sponsor:**    The Georgia Poetry Society. This competition challenged entrants to submit a poem about dogs or cats.

**Judge:**    Marissa McNamara, Decatur

**1ˢᵗ Place:**    **Rescue**
*Lynn Farmer*

**2ⁿᵈ Place:**    **Greyhound Sonnet**
*Ann Willis*

**3ʳᵈ Place:**    **Old Dog**
*Laura Anella Johnson*

## Lynn Farmer

### Rescue

My heartbeat shrieking,
races to the flutter and
the fiercely aging cry
of a fledgling's effort
to escape the helplessness,
the danger, fluffed
in wheat straw, choked
in leaf dirt, shadowed
by garage boards and
by nature's silent self.

The innocent pup in black and white
has snarled, snapped, and swatted
to challenge and to please
this plaything teasing him.
But in a breath, he is restrained,
and finch's wings are freed to fly,
empowered with a life gift
to live another day.

But Campbell-dog so soon forgets,
soon tastes of other joys,
soon calls to other flying things.

And breathless here,
exhausted by this rescue,
dripping from the humid haste,

I still can feel the aching
of an earlier evening chill:

Two years ago, we found a box
with just a toy, a can of food,
and Campbell's raven curls
of shivering silk,
whimpered low all night.

*Ann Willis*

## Greyhound Sonnet Number One

My greyhounds' legs move nothing like the wind;
Angels are far more swift in flight than they;
As champions rise, so do my hounds descend
Upon their beds, and sleep on them all day.
I've heard of beasts that hunt with stealth and skill
But no such talents see I in my dogs.
The graceful curve of swan from breast to bill
Makes my hounds' necks resemble sturdy logs.
If soaring larks sing sweet, the strangled sound
Of my three pooches' howling hurts the ears;
And there is nothing regal in a hound
Whose bony shoulders sag in later years.
And yet, by heaven, I think my hounds so rare,
Not even Shakespeare's sonnets could compare.

## Laura Anella Johnson

### Old Dog

Your pre-dawn click-clack pacing wakes me.
I find what you couldn't help but drop
in the hallway, and you in the kitchen at
the open pantry door that has blocked your path.

You stare, immobile, over dark onions and potatoes.
I bend, gingerly lift around bony rib-cage barrel.
Does your low flutter growl imply pain, or
protest removal from your confused post?

Outside, you sway, slightly stumble atop
the backyard hill you once stormed for tennis balls
again and again. I'd throw two, or three, and watch
your frantic grasping letting-go mad-dog dance.

For years, you flipped for fuzzy yellow balls,
chased squirrels or the neighbor's disrespectful cat.
Amid claw-sanding driveway darting and staccato barking,
you bristled and rebuked sirens and thunder claps.

If you meander too far down the hill this morning,
your strength won't bring you back.
I'll have to slide on sandals, retrieve you.
I open the door, cheer your four-inch hop up

our threshold step, watch you totter back to
your blanket, feel that familiar vet-office stomach dread,
and pray you'll let go on your own, lie down, unclench
your jaw, let life roll away. Leave it, Trapper, leave it.

# The Member Excellence Poetry Award

**Sponsor:**     The Georgia Poetry Society. This
                 competition challenged entrants to submit
                 their very best poetry.

**Judge:**       Rupert Fike, Atlanta

**1ˢᵗ Place:**   **Three-Mushroom Tart, Dayton,
                 Oregon**
                 *Michael Diebert*

**2ⁿᵈ Place:**   **The Hours and the God**
                 *Lynn Farmer*

**3ʳᵈ Place:**   **The Scent of a Man**
                 *Dianna Eden*

**HM:**          **Pity the Children:  Variation on a
                 Villanelle**
                 *Jill Jennings*

**HM:**          **Draining Lake Nottely**
                 *Randy Mazie*

*Michael Diebert*

---

## Three-Mushroom Tart, Dayton, Oregon

How to do right by dirt,
transliterate loam, foggy dawn,
damp hillside, plot, planet,
enormity?  How to bake it
beneath fragile, flaky layers,
control heat, calibrate
magnificence, how properly
praise this wedge of heaven
on its pristine plate, balanced
on the palm of the server
serving us all?  Now is it set
in front of me, now I see it,
nose, mouth, tongue, thus
brain, where it will burn
permanent, where earth and rain
and recall will remain perfect.
Love is like mushrooms.  Why not?
Why not us at this soft-lit table
in this refurbished restaurant
of the mind, stunned a little
at the sight?  But enough, love.
How does it taste?  Like my life.
Like ours.  Before us, before
anyone, way back, before beginning.

## Lynn Farmer

### The Hours and the God

It is not the ninth hour.
It is the nineteenth, around
Quinnie's white-robed tables.
And the crimson rimmed,
heart-shaped shadow box
plugged into the wall
holds a small clock,
with hands stretched wide,
sheltering a gold plastic Jesus
on a gold and glaring plastic cross.

He's bowing his head—fixed in agony,
in prayer, or in curiosity—to see
this supper, not the last,
piled high upon our paper plates.
Three red, fake, velvet roses spread
beneath him, large enough
to shroud his soul, one for each who died,
catching their life's color,
assuming their last, best beat
in every textured petal's veins.

This time, I can't seem
to take my eyes away,
or not for long, at least,
wondering what artist's vision
brought it all together,
studying its naïve glory,

the minutes freely given,
the hours and the god trapped
in their scentless, thornless beauty
behind a face transparent seeming
but revealing only endless passing
and a death transfixed
in all its simple and unholy innocence.

# Dianna Eden

## The Scent of a Man

She understood its dominance in her life.
Its pervasiveness, her need for it,
and the hold it held over her.
A soft blanket of warmth in winter.
The excitement of a brisk walk in fall.
A garden of stringent blooms in spring.
And the heat of her man in the summer sun.
Sometimes it enticed her.
Other times it smothered her.
Most often it soothed her.
It was what she wanted
from the one with strong arms
that held her close.
The presence of the swirl protected her.
Allowed the child to curl inside it
and the adult to satisfy her craving.
The scent was that of a man.
Her step-dad.
Both her grandpops,
Her partners.
And her best male friends.
It was the whisper of smoke from the cigarette,
the cloud curling up past half-closed eyes,
encircling hard sculpted faces.
A symbol of power. Of self-satisfaction.
Of support and protection.
A blue-white halo of strength.

It was only now, in her memories
and with gut-gripping sorrow,
she recognized the soft, alluring cloud
that enveloped her men as the
horrifying herald of death.

*Jill Jennings*

## Pity the Children:  Variation on a Villanelle

Have pity on the children of the night,
Pray they'll survive the horrors of the day.
Cruel missiles' arrows puncture morning's light,

While politicians debate wrong from right,
Sycophants with crooked smiles are they.
Have pity on the children of the night.

The Milky Way had never shone so bright,
The water now so still inside the bay,
Belie the horrors dawn reveals at light.

Once there were options, stay at home or flight,
But now all roads are ruined, there's no way.
Have pity on the children of the night.

While parents, grandparents, curse gift of sight,
Recalling better times when hearts were gay.
The future all unfurled, bright was that light.

Who dreamed the sun could fall from such a height?
Mosques, temples all in ruins, still they pray.
Have pity on the children of the night.
Cruel missiles' arrows puncture morning's light.

*Randy Mazie*

## Draining Lake Nottely

They pull the plug on the lake each fall.
It's like draining the vinyl pool after the kids
have splashed around in it all summer long.

But what it really looks like is the bathtub
my mother would find after us kids had spent
the day playing in the dirt, then another hour
that evening busily scrubbing ourselves off,
leaving a deep brown ring all around the porcelain
and caked muck all along the bottom.

Here it is now December, and the dry lake bottom
is a giant desert wasteland with its hard-cracked clay
looking like an ocher-splattered jigsaw puzzle
of amoeba-shaped pieces that no longer fit together.

Unlike my bathtub, no toys remain on the bottom of this
    bed.
All the boats are in dry dock and the floating decks are
    marooned
on the hardened clay of the summer's former shoreline.
Wooden gazebos seem to float in the air on their stilts,
and old gnarly trees strain tying to pull themselves free
from the confines of their muck-brick rooted prisons.

I walk along that graveyard of a lake and I imagine the spirits
of warm-weather children laughing, swimming and splashing,
the illusory humming of watercraft cruising speedily by,
and the eerie visions of bobbing fishing poles waving to me
from scattered johnboats moored upon the once-proud lake.

I wish I could have been around to see them pull the plug.
Somewhere on the bottom, I'm sure, is this monstrous
black rubber stopper hooked to an imposing chain-link
connected to a mighty winch which click-clacks slowly
until the tiniest slit opens between the stopper and the lakebed,
when *whoosh,* the stopper is driven violently back and up,
propelled by the weight of the drowning lake rushing
down and out to where all the world's dirty bathwater goes
       when it is all used up and no longer needed.

# Member Poems

# *Roland Caissie*

## Confessional

In the confessional
of this examination table, flesh
left naked as my soul,
cold polygraphic tests expose

heart's pressure,
pulse, contaminated
corpuscles
and body heat…

All secrets told,
no holding back
the sin
of weekend gin

or hidden smoke consumption, lack
of exercise, too many sweets,
a long-forgotten,
unprotected dalliance…

2
Whatever's there
they'll see,
and there's no rosary
of rote Our Father's prated

or Hail Mary's droned
that grants me absolution.
Here,
all sin is mortal, and

the sister of mercy
nurse who's knotted
up my arm and now
in silence stands

extracting every bit of blood
I've got appears
indifferent
to my *mea culpas*.

*Steven Croft*

## Miracles

morning songs of birds
in their different languages,
beautiful Babel

the moon laying
its dancing silver reflection
on a dark sea

pines whispering news
of winter, sparks lighting wood smoke
stirring like bees

spring explosions of flowers
in sunshine, a quiet gardener's
joy

# *Nancy Degenhardt*

## Coming

In my seventy-sixth year
I left the earth
My lungs were used up
My heart worn out

I had to go alone
When I entered the earth
I was not alone
I was in a body
In which I grew into a man
I accumulated things
Clothes, cars, money
Now I had to leave them behind

I thought of something
I could take my memories
But a powerful voice spoke
You cannot take them
They will be placed in a box
To be opened when you
Stand before God

I soared alone
Through the heavens
Higher than I had ever
Gone before awaiting
My future

*Norma Duncan*

## Leaving Home

Slave traders attacked
village in black of night

Captured, forced into temporary
quarters, lower-level brig of
slave ship

Bodies side by side, alternating
Positions, form inhumane body designs
Holes, slits in wood reveals
natures day, natures night

Stench from bodily waste obstructs
breathing passages

Children, adults, secured by shackles
Leg irons clank haunting sounds
Sea movement beats against ship

Eyes open to darkness once again
I pray "Lord take me, take me."

Hungry child snuggles to my breast
Movement to upper deck induces bodily pain

Water thrown against bodies, first in months
Mush shoved into mouths like slop to pigs

Leg irons allow slow foot movement
toward edge of boat

Cold sea water greets body, arms
wrap tightly around baby

Thirst, pain, hunger erased
Now free to be with God

# Edward Gadrix

## The Rising

Coffins pack corpses of countrymen's souls
Once walked this earth with footprints of bold.
Packed coffins pack trailers to stem the tide
Of parades of countrymen who lost and died.
                    Rising, rising, not surprising.

Fellows from families who no longer wonder
How their lives will be torn asunder.
Hearts still beating say their goodbyes
Through gadgets and windows with tears in their eyes.
                    Rising, rising, not surprising.

Cold, parked tailers align all together
Like solders in rank to salute and gather.
Departed souls whose silence within
Lay still—they wait—eventual end.
                    Rising, rising, not surprising.

There is no beauty for them in such death;
There is no funeral to remember their breath.
They stay still in a cold, dark trailer
Among fellow travelers to be with forever.
                    Rising, rising, not surprising.

They never knew the early flu,
They share the past; they share the rue.
And life beyond is only reward
For a meager life, here, probably bored.
                Rising, rising, not surprising.

Ignorance, incompetence is the real cause
By a leaderless Mouthpiece who has no laud
For anyone departed, their station's below.
The bluster of Mouthpiece is his own foe.
                Rising, rising, not surprising.

Half a mil, half of mil the bodies keep rising;
The goal not reached by Mouthpiece's lying.
But fate, too, has goals to pay debt;
Owed to those who caused such deaths.
                Rising, rising, not surprising.

Corpses stand tall with hands outstretched
Beckoning Mouthpiece and those of his fetch.
He—they—will differ in space;
They will not see them, their body, their face.

He—they—will not touch hands outstretched;
There is no rising for Mouthpiece and fetch.

# Emory Jones

## Sacred Music

*A gloss on lines from "The Aeolian Harp" by Samuel Taylor Coleridge*

Methinks it should have been impossible
Not to love all things in a world so filled;
Where the breeze warbles and the mute still air
Is Music slumbering on her instrument

Methinks it should have been impossible
Not to feel the rhythm of the spheres,
The joyous music of the Lord's which still
In undertones so permeates our ears--
Methinks it should have been impossible

Not to love all things in a world so filled
With symphonies of His created score
With chords so firm and melody that's trilled
By every living thing that we adore--
Not to love all things in a world so filled

Where the breeze warbles, and the mute still air
Is but the pause before the music swells
Again in great crescendo of our prayer
Of praise to Him from everyone who dwells
Where the breeze warbles, and the mute still air

Is Music slumbering on her instrument
In dreams of the eternal song to Him
Who orchestrates the harmonies He meant
    To elevate our souls--our silent hymn
    Is Music slumbering on her instrument.

## Laurie Smith Jones

### Atlanta Haiku:  Sunrise in My City

spires, the city tops
a deepening pink backdrop
bed of pines below

# Lou Jones

## The Busboy Poet

I have only felt free through my writing, released from
any who would own my life. I draw on truth as my heart
leads me to it, call humanity out from the shadows
into the light — sacred commitments not for hire. Today
I celebrate. I renew my dreams, too long deferred.

Yes ma'am,
I celebrate, am buying myself a new suit of clothes.
I know what I want, *Brooks Brothers*, double-breasted, beige,
no pinstripes, must be plain beige. I want quality at an
honest price, payin' with dollars *I* earned. An unpretentious
garment that conveys the soft tone of my new life.
I'll wear the suit often, complemented by the finest
cordovan oxfords, cloth-buffed to a high sheen.

I will stroll Harlem in the new ensemble — past
Jackson's Bar and Poolroom, colliding pool balls
competing with street noises, odors of cigar smoke and
stale brew escaping through café doors. I'll visit
Curb Market with its tiers of tropical fruits and vegetables,
flares of color reaching out to the white sky. I'll make my
way down Restaurant Row, savor the aromas drifting from
eatery kitchens and tamale carts. I will stop by the
bocce courts, paisans in fedoras drinkin' beer from
growlers, shouting "hit the pallino, hit the pallino."

On Strivers' Row I'll strike a stately carriage, imagine
the fine life, greet the good folks with a nod and a smile.
I will amble like I'm but another face in the crowd,
little to set me apart, the beige suit expressing
detachment, my manner of being among but not of.

Early evening I will saunter over to the club. Bessie's
droppin' in. It will be a blues free-for-all. I'll grab a
table, order a man's sippin' drink, relax, take in the
*Empress of the Blues* decorating the room with genius.

As the night sounds drop into silence, I will follow
the streetlights home, look back on the day, satisfied.

Yes ma'am —
a contented man in a beige suit. In time it could become
my favorite — it might be the suit I'm sportin' the first time
I meet friends for luncheon at the *Waldorf-Astoria.*

## Nancy Kollock

### Beech Trees

In the bleak midwinter,
Some trees lift bare branches skyward.
Beech trees cling to translucent leaves
And tiptoe through the woods
Like fragile little old ladies,
Undaunted.

## Brenda Kay Ledford

### Toast the Season

On this bleak winter day,
fog shrouds Wolf Mountain,
gray clouds smother the earth,
naked poplar trees shiver

in the whistling wind.
Lichen covers the drooping
limbs of the dogwood,
creatures teem Chattahoochee River.

The red-tailed hawk
soars above the rocky shoals
with hope as the sun
sets the horizon on fire.

A dark road grows
brighter as spring arrives,
purple violets dance in the vineyard,
toast the season with wine.

*Susan Lindsley*

## Facing Our Winter

Let's sit together on the porch and watch the bluebirds fly
And hand-in-hand go strolling as the sunset paints the sky.

Let's sit together in the swing and hear the whip-o-wills
And in the early spring let's pick a thousand daffodils.

Let's wander deep into the woods where wild azaleas grow
And stroll together down the trails where deer and bunnies go.

Let's listen for the gobbling from the pines up on the hill
And snuggle by the fire to ward off early autumn chill.

Winter lies so close ahead, our autumn soon is gone,
So let us live and love and laugh while we are flesh and bone.

*Donna Rose Mulcahy*

## Rita Cecelia O'Connor

Crystal beauty glides across the carpeted stage.
Her bathing bloomers render the living room crowd
to hushed amaze.
Slow pivot turn,
graceful wave,
signals my turn to take the stage.
Petite braided beauty
in her little girl bikini
imitates the sashay, gaze, wave.
Slow pivot-turn to exit the stage.
Grandma and I
put the TV contestants to shame.

# Ed Nichols

## Tribute To Byron Herbert Reece

I never knew you, but I came so very close.
You died in June, just a few steps from the dorm
room I moved to in August.
I lived and studied for two years, only a few feet
from the room where your life ended.
I so wish you could have stayed for a while longer.

Perhaps I would have gained the knowledge of poetry
that I so wanted, so needed.
Instead, it has taken me a lifetime to learn.
I still struggle with words in lines, in verses,
like you achieved with perfect rhyme and rhythm.
I have studied you, read all your creations, visualized
you as the renowned long-legged farmer,
lover of your parents, lover of nature, lover of words.

I often revisit the "Ballard of the Bones."
Study nature, read the Bible, still trying to learn
how to write, how to find words like you withdrew
from the waters of Wolf Creek.
Words like you planted in "The Valley Green With Corn."

I visualize you reading and writing beneath dim fireplace
light in the little family farmhouse in Choestoe Valley.
Going to California, teaching, remembering
your mother from such a long distance. Teaching
at Emory and Young Harris, suffering from the family
affliction, and accepting faithful death on your doorstep.

I wish I had at least been there listening to Mozart with you that last day. Most of all, I wish you had not been beyond the reach of song when I arrived on campus, so many years ago.

# Kathryn Schmeiser

## A Beauty Berry Speaks

I wriggle my roots
in damp soil.

It is a mystery how
I landed *here* and
avoided sprouting
in the middle of
those pink-tousled
weeds.

Did I begin life
  as a tiny seed
    tumbling
      down
        a slope?

My journey came
to a halt
next to an unfeeling concrete
wall, one that suppresses
stretching my branches.

I am here.

Until today.

You disturb my
daydream
with loosening
earth, nudging me
from my dwelling
with a cold metal
spade.

I've put down roots,
you know.

## Tanya R. Whitney

### Quiet Sounds

Yellow winged butterflies flutter
among the red and orange petals
of the mountain meadows.

Delicate wisps that sway
in the winds sweeping down
from the craggy mountains.

Sitting upon the bank of the lake
gazing out over the water with eyes
closed to the bright sun.

I feel the breath of God across my
face as I lift my head high
toward the heavens.

There is no sound in the glade
to disturb my soul or to
interrupt my meditation.

The day passes quickly as I
soak in the solitude of this meadow
nestled amidst the mountains.

The sun begins to dip behind
the ridges of the ragged tops
surrounding the solitude.

The quiet whispers of day's end
whispers across the grasslands and
in the silent rustling of the trees.

The sounds of the hushed day will
soon change to those of the night as
the stillness of the night brings peace.

# George C. Williams III

## Walking Man

As he crosses the street in front of me
I take no special note
He is doing what he always does,
walking all over town
Looking away without concern
I continue on my way
But, glancing back, I see him pause
and stare into a bin of trash
Curious now, I watch him as
he turns and walks away
Goes on to another trash bin,
where he stops and stares again
Never saw him do that before
Something in his life has changed
They say he was normal once,
then, one day, he lost his way
when his wife left and broke his heart
He's never been the same since then,
started walking all over town
Never speaks or even looks at you
as if you don't exist
Until today I thought, perhaps,
He may have been looking for her
But now I wonder if this wandering soul
Is searching for himself

## *Ann Willis*

### Festive Day

My photos came today
and, with them, the shock of
your eyes
caught in private sadness
by the careless lens
on that festive day
when I had thought we were all smiling.

## Kimberly Wright

### Use Alternate Route

The sound of impact brought me
careening back from sleep,
the highway less than a mile away,
jolted my pets, scattering peace as we

listened, prone, for what came next,
sirens shrieking across the gloom.
What drove us from sleep manifested
in two brief PD tweets the next day—one

alerting motorists to a multi-vehicle accident
blocking the intersection of Main and Highway 92—
"use alternate route," followed by a brief note
the way was clear. Garden-variety mishaps

don't garner much press. Watch out
for catastrophe, higher body count. Look—
a fireball incinerated two when a tanker
struck a woman's car stalled on the interstate.

Petroleum infiltrated drains and fire
spread through sewers, blasting
manhole covers, forcing people from office.
The horrific demands stories

and follow-ups. Chain-reaction leakage
of bad luck wends into cobwebs,
seeps through leaky windows
settles on the comforter like cold.

Concussion waves strike deep,
but soon enough, you'll pass a fuel truck
and not feel the heat rise up.

# Robert Wyatt

## Star Trails

Only by inspecting time-lapse photographs
can we discern movement of the stars,
which, in fact, are fixed in the firmament.
It is we who actually are in motion,
riding this ball we call Earth,
rotating on its axis, journeying around the sun.
Only the North Star appears not to move,
a reckoning point for navigation in our hemisphere.

Only by scrutinizing photographs of ourselves
as we grow older can we observe how we age:
how flesh sags, wrinkles appear, and hair
changes color, retreats, and eventually vanishes.
Inside we may feel no different at all.
Our soul— our essence— remains intact,
serving as our guiding light,
our lodestar, steering us to our destiny.

# Contributors

**Roland Caissie**. Doraville, GA. Previous poems published in small outlets when he lived overseas, since for personal expression and private consumption.

**Nancy Cook**. St. Paul, MN. Coordinates the "Witness Project," a series of free community writing workshops in Minneapolis designed to enable creative work by underrepresented voices, and, as an artist affiliate for the Southwest Minnesota Housing Authority, helps design arts programs for adults in transitional housing.

**Steven Croft**. Saint Simons Island, GA. *Moment and Time* (The Saltmarsh Press, 2015); *New World Poems* (Alien Buddha Press, 2020). *Williwaw Journal, Canary, The New Verse News, San Pedro River Review.*

**doris davenport**. Sautee Nacoochee, GA. Twelve books of poetry. Latest collection: *dancing in time* (2019). Ph.D. in African American literature from the University of Southern California.

**Nancy Degenhardt**. Atlanta, GA. *Stephen's Gift* (independently published).

**Michael Diebert**. Avondale Estates, GA. *Life Outside the Set* (Sweatshoppe, 2013). *Another Chicago Magazine, jmww, Free State Review.*

**Norma J. Duncan**. West Palm Beach, FL. *Reach of Song, Poet of the Palm Beaches.*

**Dianna Eden**. Atlanta, GA. *Reach of Song.*

**Lynn Farmer**. Decatur, GA. *The Rare, Persistent Light* (Georgia Poetry Society, 2012). *Lullwater Review, Chattahoochee Review, Red Mountain Rendezvous, Snake Nation Review.* Edward Davin Vickers Award, Byron Herbert Reece International Award, James E. Warren Prize, Charles Dickson Chapbook Award 2011, Chattahoochee Valley Writers' Award, Ron Boggs Memorial Poetry Award.

**Edward Gadrix**. Roswell, GA. First publication.

**David Hutto**. Gainesville, GA. *I'd Tear Down the Stars* (short story collection), *The Illusion of Being Here* (novel).

**Jill Jennings**. Ft. Myers, FL. Books: *Pineapple Wine: Poems of Maui* (2019); *The Poetry Alarm Clock* (2012); *Dead Man's Flower* (2008). *Atlanta Review, Oberon Review, Reach of Song, Encore, KSU's Poetry of The Golden Generation, Please See Me.*

**Laura Anella Johnson**. Sharpsburg, GA. *The Color of Truth* (Kelsay Books, in press), *Not Yet* (Kelsay Books, 2019). *Snakeskin, Heart of Flesh, Tipton, The Other Journal.*

**Emory D. Jones**. Iuka, MS. *Writer's Digest, Falling Star Magazine, Free Xpressions Magazine, The Storyteller, Modern Poetry Quarterly Review, Gravel, Pasques Petals, The Pink Chameleon, and Encore: Journal of the NFSPS.*

**Laura Smith Jones**. Marietta, GA.

**Lou Jones**. Pooler, GA. *So You Want to Be a Poet* (iUniverse, 2019), *After the Blast* (iUniverse, 2016), *From Microbe to Consciousness* (iUniverse, 2009). *Oconee Living, Seasons on Lake Oconee, Reach of Song.*

**Nancy Kollock**. Clarkesville, GA. First publication.

**Brenda Kay Ledford**. Hayesville, NC. *Reagan's Romps* (Kelsay Books, 2021); *Red Plank House* (Kelsay Books, 2018); *Crepe Roses (*Aldrich, 2014), *Beckoning* (Finishing Line Press, 2013). *Our State, Appalachian Heritage, Asheville Poetry Review, Town Creek Poetry, Mysterious Ways, The Broad River Review.*

**Susan Lindsley**. Decatur and Milledgeville, GA. *When Yestertime Was Now* (ThomasMax Publishing, 2020); *Whisper of Love* (ThomasMax Publishing 2020); *Christmas Gift* (self-published), *O Yesterplace* (1999, self-published). *Reach of Song.*

**Randy Mazie**. Blairsville, GA. *The Anthology of Transcendent Poetry* (Cosmographia Books, 2019). *The MacGuffin, DASH.*

**Donna Rose Mulcahy**. Atlanta, GA. *Reach of Song.*

**Ed Nichols**. Eatonton, GA. *I Wish I Could Laugh* (independently published, 2020). *One Art, Ariel Chart International Journal, The Literary Yard, Belle Reve Literary Journal.*

**Clela Reed**. Athens, GA. Seven collections of poetry, recently *Silk* (Evening Street Press, 2019), which won the Helen Kay Chapbook Prize and the 2020 Georgia Author of the Year chapbook competition. *Cortland Review, Southern Poetry Review, The Atlanta Review, Valparaiso Review, The Literati Review, Clapboard House.*

**Kathryn (Kit) Schmeiser**.  Fairview, NC. *The Reach of Song, The Tower.*

**Kimberly Simms**. Palmetto, GA.  *Lindy Lee:  Songs on Mill Hill* Finishing Line, 2017).  *Aji Magazine, Broad River Review, Poem, The South Carolina Review, The Asheville Poetry Review, Eclipse* and others.  2016 Carl Sandburg National Historic Site Writer-in-Residence and scholar on the SC Humanities Council's speaker's bureau. Her work is included in the South Carolina Poetry Archives at Furman University.

**Tanya R. Whitney**.  Sorrento, LA.  *A Soldier's Journey Home* (independently published, 2021).  *Reach of Song, Treasures Found in a Cedar Chest, Sandcutters, Ink to Paper.*

**George C. Williams III**.  Madison, GA.  *Lake Oconee Magazine, Morgan County Citizen, Mamie, Magnolia, Melissa, Reach of Song.*

**Ann Willis**.  Clarkesville, GA.  *River of Words, Volume 2* (2016 anthology); *The Reach of Song 2018, 2019, 2020.*

**Kimberly Wright**.  Woodstock, GA.  *Not Pictured* (Finishing Line Press, 2020.) *Poydras Review, Eunoia Review, UCity Review, October Hill Magazine.*

**Robert Wyatt**. Bishop, GA.  *Inner Chords, Reach of Song, Yellowthroat.*

# Ann Willis

## Georgia Poetry Society Year in Review: 2020

<u>January 2020: The 164th Meeting</u>

The first Georgia Poetry Society meeting of 2020 was held at the Decatur-Dekalb County Library on Saturday, January 25$^{th}$. It opened with the installation of new officers and Board members: Steven Shields as president, Alyson Shields as vice president, and John Ottley and Ann Willis as new Board members. Continuing were Lyn Hopper as treasurer and Ann Gillespie as secretary, and Board members Kristin Gorell, Ed Hall, and Andrea Jurjevic.

Multi-award-winning poet Jericho Brown was the featured reader for the morning. In addition to reading, he shared inspiring stories, including of his library experience as a child. Brown's presentation was enthusiastically received by a larger than usual gathering of attendees, which included several non-members. Afterwards, he signed copies of his latest collection, *The Tradition* (longlisted for the National Book Award). Six members of The Side Door Poets writing-and-critique group graced the stage in the afternoon to present an eclectic and entertaining selection of poems. Reading were Karen Paul Holmes, Ricks Carson, Dan Veach, Rupert Fike, Trish Percival, and Jim Langford. GPS had launched a group membership initiative late in 2019, and The Side Door Poets group was the first to take advantage of this.

## April 2020: The 165th Meeting

In March 2020, COVID-19 suddenly emerged as a significant and life-changing public health threat. It quickly spread across the world. In Georgia, a Public Health State of Emergency was declared on March 14th and schools were ordered to close a few days later. On March 24th, in addition to many other restrictions being announced, a shelter-in-place for certain categories of people was decreed and a limit was set in Georgia for all public gatherings. The spring meeting scheduled for April 25th had to be cancelled.

In late spring, Jericho Brown, our January meeting reader, was announced as winner of the 2020 Pulitzer Prize for Poetry for *The Tradition*. GPS members took two prizes in the Georgia Author of the Year Awards for Poetry, chapbook category: Clela Reed in first place with *Silk,* and Diana Anhalt as finalist with *Walking Backward*.

## July 2020:  The 166th Meeting

When it became clear in early summer that the pandemic had taken hold and was worsening, with no end in sight, GPS president Steven Shields organized a Virtual Quarterly Meeting for July 25th. James Green, winner of the 2019 Charles Dickson Chapbook Contest, was featured poet, reading from his winning chapbook, *Long Journey Home*, of which the theme was a revision and revisiting of ancient myths. Greg Emilio, winner of the coveted $1000 single prize for the Byron Herbert Reece Competition, the only general competition offered in the 2019 cycle, read his poem "For Everything in Paradise." The three members who placed in the Member Excellence contest also read their poems.

A survey was distributed during late summer to gauge member preferences as to how the upcoming fall contest cycle should be structured. Based on feedback, the number of contests for fall 2020 was reset with more contests and more modest prizes. One of the new contests added was on the topic of social issues, named for former GPS president Ira E. Harrison. A new chapbook contest named for former president Ron Self, funded with donations in his memory, was established to run in alternate years from the Charles Dickson Chapbook Contest.

### October 2020: The 167th Meeting

Julie E. Bloemeke was guest poet at the Fall Quarterly Meeting, held again via Zoom, on October 24th; she read from her newly published collection, *Slide to Unlock*. Member reader Laura Johnson read from her 2019 poetry book, *Not Yet*.

### Addenda

The Georgia Poetry Society remembers two past presidents who passed away in 2020: Ira E. Harrison and Ron Self.

Also remembered is Bob Lynn, a dedicated and active volunteer with GPS, who served as editor of *The Reach of Song*.

Mildred White Greear, former longtime Georgia Poetry Society member, celebrated her 100th birthday in Helen, Georgia, on October 19, 2020.

## *About the Georgia Poetry Society*

The Georgia Poetry Society is a volunteer nonprofit organization dedicated to the craft and performance of poetry. We offer readings by published poets and workshops at quarterly meetings held in January, April, July and October around the state of Georgia. Meetings are free and open to anyone interested in poetry. Each meeting features at least one open mic opportunity for members to read their works to us. We publish this annual anthology, *The Reach of Song*, featuring member works and contest-winning poets, as well as an annual chapbook series. Further information is to be found on our website at www.georgiapoetrysociety.org.

# Index of Contributors

www.ingramcontent.com/pod-product-compliance
Lightning Source LLC
Chambersburg PA
CBHW051308250626
47155CB00009B/3484